THE END OF AMERICA

BOOK FIFTEEN

MARK WALLACE

THE END OF AMERICA

BOOK FIFTEEN

MARK WALLACE

The End of America, Book Fifteen
Copyright © 2021 Mark Wallace

First Edition, Glovebox Poems
ISBN: 978-1-943899-13-5

Design by Adam Deutsch

All rights reserved. No part of this book may be reproduced without the publisher's written permission, except for brief quotations in reviews.

A hand slaps a grimy glass window. The hand goes quickly past the glass. Smear of four fingerprints, pinky hovering absent. Lingering smudge.

Blue trees and green ducks line the white rows between the blue rows (sweater).

Door, a word on a sign, a truck.

The arm lowers, raises, lowers, raises, not touching anything beneath or above it.

Fantasies of being something other are also part of oneself. Yet being oneself is made up of all the things not oneself.

Kansas rock band sweatshirt as a backdrop for earphones.

Advertisement: "It's That Simple."

White patch flashes out from black uniform. Color gets lost in the human-order color scheme.

Sidewalk, one voice in Arabic, ten in English.

The tiger in the painting has a square building made of blue trees on its skin, walks away from the blue and white checkerboard leopard, looks back at a field of red, orange, blue. The red, orange, and blue human bodies lie slaughtered on a long strip of black.

Mom talking on cellphone grabs hand of boy in shorts before they cross the street.

Dent in the side of a Corvette vanishes when the sun glare does.

Slender, shiny black running shoes.

Click of a camera starts the video, bright lower edge reading time 9:58:24, gun muzzle like one side of a triangle, everything now running for the recording of the shooting that will put him on TV.

The wire folds out over a wheel and shapes itself into a laundry cart.

Blue betta fish gazes, fascinated, at a gnat clinging to the side of the bowl.

The dream does not parallel anything outside it.

Stacks of plastic bags, rows of garbage cans.

Global blank.

Wall of hot air.

The metallic shrieking is a narrowing idea.

The traffic cone, a twenty questions answer, lies smashed in the road as the driver stares, confused, at the long orange row.

The burden of noticing turns into the burden of refusing to notice.

The benches under the pounding sun sit empty. There are no benches in the shade.

Abstract, it digs under the skin like a pebble in a shoe.

"Gravitate towards Jupiter": a sticker on the wall in the coffee shop bathroom.

The second gate is the correct entrance for the Goodwill Drop-Off Center.

Gold clock hung upside down on a white wall.

Brief glimpse of the back wheel of a bike as it goes out a door.

"I'm sick of it!" she shouts at passing cars from a sidewalk beneath construction scaffolding.

One man, then two, then three, sit on a torn couch.

His splotchy red bald head, bright red shirt, and turned-down now-quiet mouth once talked loudly drunk at me at a party I barely remember.

On the sidewalk, one human hand after another holds a rope attached to the collar of one dog after another.

In front of a white roof, some green leaves and yellow flowers sway under the sun. In front of the green leaves and yellow flowers in the sun, some green leaves sway in shadow. In front of the green leaves in shadow stand metal bars, motionless, black.

The men all wear shirts with numbers on them, each number different.

Plastic cola bottle in a bush. The sound of sweeping.

Question? Silence. Question? Silence.

Days after the system shutdown ends, resentment about the shutdown surges along the shoulders and the backs of the eyes.

Relief comes, even laughter, when a device starts functioning again.

Ambulance lights, spinning in place, flash in the window of each car driving past.

Brown dress shoes click across the floor, leaving a metallic echo behind them, where before the only sound had been an increasing mass of distant voices beyond a glass door.

Undercurrent under the undercurrent leaps up, lashes, divides.

You are not the person, walking, who everyone can see. You are the person, walking behind that person, who no one can see.

The wide desk is empty. The chairs sit so low that the wide desk cannot be used.

The fence boards lie in the grass. The shed lock lies in the grass, shed doors open. The man lies on the gravel next to the grass, yelling that he wants to fight. The police take him away.

"Yes," they all say, nodding, "that's me, in the picture, looking at me in the picture."

Now lean against, lean hard and you won't fall.

Cranes rise high, lights blinking, above the highway bridge.

Ownership of boats is another clue.

Somewhere, infractions are being counted.

The guard walks around restlessly, stops beside people, talks to them.

Flat facades of colored apartment blocks, still being constructed: red, white, yellow, white, blue, white, grey. No glass in any of the windows.

Chairs sit at haphazard angles around the room, people in a few of them, none looking at each other.

The brown dog, mostly quiet, barks when other dogs pass.

Just past dawn, three men in the fog laugh as they walk towards the golf course.

On the left, a fence. A fence on the right. The only path is straight ahead.

Heavy sun against the face curdles the stomach.

Each of the group has a different story about air-conditioning bills.

What a scene is depends on the angle and distance from which you watch it.

A pile of white socks with black stripes.

He says, "I haven't sat on a chair this comfortable in years."

The Hilton trademark "H" commands the horizon.

A hand pushes a flashlight into a bag.

The eyelids droop. The head, under a hat, falls forwards towards the table at a spot between two books.

Beneath the lamps, the faces look down, or up, to the left or right, anywhere except at another face.

It becomes imperative—for no reason at all—to mention the big white clock face with red hands on the tower overlooking the bay.

The computer contains requests for things to be done, signed with names.

The comments quote philosophers in the debate about what to stamp out.

"I'm sorry to offend you," he says to the woman with a nose-ring behind the coffee shop counter.
"You didn't offend me." She shakes her head. "I'm just in work mode."
He drops his yoga mat.
She turns to the next customer.

Coffee cups, water bottles, plastic and glass, clear and not clear. Miniature cacti in pots.

Inhale three seconds. Exhale three seconds. Notice your body. Notice where you are.

A soft gelatin.

Sun flashes through the weave of the mat shaken out over the railing by an unseen person.

For example, say someone cuts you off in traffic.

Each time a plane comes over, the roar grows slowly in the sky.

Seeing a man ahead of her on the sidewalk, looking around as if he's lost something, the teenage girl crosses to the other side of the street.

It's the simulation of a town with people living in it like a town.

Every image falls short of a description of what's there, dusty green towel in the dirt, hawk overhead.

In a t-shirt, she sits on the counter in the retail store. A cashier walks up and says, "Can I help you?"
"I'm with them." She points to a family standing in front of another counter. "We've been here a long time."

In the rainstorm, water flies up from the road and blurs out everything else. A few minutes later on the same road, the sun between buildings blurs out everything else.

The quaver starts in the legs and moves up.

Four of them lean down over the table, looking at each other, no one speaking.

The present instantly becomes the past. The past no longer exists. The future never arrives.

Many remarks are made about the beauty of the location.

After dark, the bicycle taxis flash with spinning wheel-lights, circling past the resort hotels.

"I would like a boat," he says to a friend as they walk past storefronts.

Hands wave at each other from opposite sides of the street.

A lot hinges on whether one thinks some other one might actually be listening.

Two pairs of shoes on a rack. Six hats on the floor.

Corner left, an image of a small lighted bulb with short lines of light extending out. The top of a steering wheel stands below a darkening twilight. Otherwise, the usually lighted panel is dark. Through the window behind the panel, car lights flash white, searing. Car lights in front of the panel go periodically red. Gradually, the dark outline of hills blends and finally vanishes into the sky. Lights in the distance on the sides of the roads may be from houses where strangers live.

They are not coming, one by one or in groups, to get or save anyone.

At the meeting about the party, the meeting organizer refers to the spouses and children of the office workers (more than half of whom are women) as "widows and orphans."

"I feel bad about it, and it's embarrassing."
    "Well just don't tell me then."

The dark patch of shade under tightly bunched trees in front of the Catholic Church social hall retreats as the afternoon goes on.

"Drugs used to execute convicted murderers are regulated by laws that vary from state to state."

The wind passes through the afternoon trees with a soft consistent hum.

The only crow in the sky caws three times, black wings disappearing beneath an apartment roof.

The old man, stooped over, slowly pushes a grocery cart stuffed with bags stuffed with clothes. He reaches a park bench, stops, sits. Out of one of the bags he pulls a paperback and begins to read.

Fence, gate, padlock. Clear plastic sheeting thrown over them all.

The momentary sharp sensation of the needle jabs half an inch into the arm.

Two anonymous Internet identities argue and insult each other furiously over their commitment to events that are not taking place.

Comfort washes through the stomach at the barely audible sound of lawnmowers.

Not up, not down, not fast, not slow, not bright, not dim, not loud, not quiet, not hard, not soft, not cold, not hot.

One name plate taped over another and another and another decorates the mailbox.

The grey sheet, twisted several times around, lies half off the bed and trails down along the floor.

Choosing the right moment in someone's rant to interrupt or walk away.

Zoom in on the stage. Zoom in more. More. Is that a hand? A string? A chin?

Post-revolutionary homes and gardens.

A glitch in abstract space leads to a dead stop in three-dimensional space.

In the creek bed, there's no creek and no bed. Fading leaves.

Who creates the app that marks the woman beside the bridge as a woman who has no home?

Alongside each thing that is, the ghostly presence of the thing it could have been does not hover.

Two black shirts move side by side down the street, only one with letters spelling Nike and the curved swoosh symbol.

"I'm not the kind who likes to tell you."

The songs coming through the space of the shop imply that the motions of people walking through have been choreographed for a musical collage.

Sometimes the skin feels like the cool afternoon air could bruise it or pop it open.

House window, car window, chat window, window to the stars.

The empty bench sits behind five three-foot concrete pillars, designed maybe to keep cars from driving up the sidewalk.

A lot of events are not expected and do not fit any plan.

Structuralism, stereotype.

Not how to not know what is known, but how to know it differently.

The jets pop and roar, unseen, above the roofs of city apartments.

Two knees show through pre-torn jeans.

The folded, soiled dollar bill flutters against a lamppost in the wind.

As if the perfected concept of landscape was one from which people had been removed?

Wind slaps the branches of a bush against a fence.

The house is painted the color of a pumpkin.

Fingers stretching, the skin on the backs of the fingers grows grooved. Rings of the tree.

Strikethrough or underline?

Numbers slip, constantly, in and out of the total.

Noted.

The difference between the 15 ticks of 15 seconds and the room that sits quietly, dark except for the light of a single lamp.

Hands click across keyboards in an underground office and determine where the collected art will or will not be found.

Red letters on the side of a truck parked on a bridge: "Jesus Christ is Lord, ot a swear word," the N inexplicably erased.

"No purpose any longer discernible."

"Shut me off / because I go crazy / with this planet / in my hands."

The flat, calm shade beneath a stone wall, two white plastic chairs nearby, empty.

The man killed seven people in four states over a five-year period. Twenty years later, he is killed by the state of Kansas.

Beyond the row of houses on a hillside sits a row of houses on a higher hillside.

The question of who locates meaning where.

Painted across the hulls: Dalena, Coyote, Barbara H, Her Grace, Three Boys, Nancy, Four C's, Lydorien, Millie G.

Wistful saxophone soundtrack moves across the water between the sounds of shoes of runners and walkers along the shore sidewalk.

The possibility of feeling trapped by what's not present.

The back of a seal floats out above the water and, between the pylons, back under.

The red velvet plush cushion seat on a bicycle cab momentarily blocks out the view of people's passing shoulders.

The dog, barking, lips pulled back, teeth out, charges the delivery van in the road. The van slides past it. The dog sees a runner on the sidewalk and, determined to show a control that neither of them has, charges the man and stops in front of him, barking again, teeth out.

Frequently, bystanders say that they watched the event like they were watching a movie.

How many feel themselves doing rather than being done to?

Deport them, a man shouts.

Picking shoes to go with pants or pants to go with shoes?

All the cars and trucks, at all five points (one from a parking lot) leading into the intersection, sit without moving.

A quivering panic begins in the chest.

Long gold streaks (rust?) drop down the sides of the white hull.

The shining red and white of the football jerseys flicker off and against each other with the movement of the men sitting on and hovering around the outdoor bar stools.

Two women lean against a fence on the edge of the underside of a bridge, talking, one with her elbows on the fence.

A man's black beard sticks out from the open side door of a van.

The head of a man passes under the doorway and into the background, bringing the doorway into the foreground.

A bottle cap sits on the otherwise empty picnic table.

Air vent, extension cord, door mat.

On the street of empty (for now) sleeping bags and tents, a lone man sits on a rickety chair, swiping at an iPhone.

Many new terraces are being built quickly.

Sedate state.

Hanging from the back of a crane as it turns across the skyline: a U.S. flag nearly a hundred feet long.

Down a level, up a level, down two levels, up two levels.

The guard tells a man in a chair at the library to keep his eyes open. The guard walks away and the man's eyes shut again. Then, later, they open, glaring at the afternoon sun beyond the high windows.

Under what seems a motivation lies another motivation.

Three steel beams lean against each other.

In another city, one that is many cities, that has a name that is many names, the buildings rise up on the far side of the water, shadowy buildings in the white light of a white cloud, cranes in the foreground, sailboats in the foreground of the cranes. Nearby there's the rumble of a train, of a truck clunking over the train track, and there's a bench and one small pine tree, sharply green, which hides someone who can barely be seen. Among it all, the unknown, as it always does, hovers as part of what's not there.

The big houses are photographed and the photos are put on paper and the paper is taped inside the window that has letters on it reading "Real Estate."

Hello boat with nobody on it. Where have you been?

As if subjectivity will make it bearable.

Those who can identify trees and their own connections to trees are closer to the world around them.

When selecting cash back, be careful to push the correct debit button.

The man gets out of the truck and picks up, from the truck bed, several landscaping tools and crosses the manicured grass towards the barracks.

A fence goes up and around the just-abandoned Goodwill Retail Store.

The dark windows of the houses on a cloudy afternoon suggest how many details of the lives inside each house remain hidden.

Consider for an instant that the hummingbird, emitting a nearly metallic high-pitched buzz, views this scene of flowering trees differently than the humans walking down the street.

Very little is clear about the relation between perceiver and perceived.

An array of opinions swirls around the issue of whether to remain in, or change, the situation.

A plastic coffee cup lid sits in the road.

A plastic straw lies in the grass.

A handmade sign reading "Fight Back" leans against a fire hydrant.

The word "Sign" is wheat-pasted on a sidewalk.

A clear plastic bag flutters across a road.

A balloon is tied to a fence post.

A traffic cone sits on a park bench.

A coat in the dirt looks trampled.

A paper plate has been balled up and dropped on a tree trunk.

Cigarette butts are tossed on the sidewalk, block after block.

A filled trash bag lies ripped in the road on a bridge.

An empty wallet is stuffed in an empty flower pot.

A "Do Not Cross" sign is propped on a window.

A pair of torn wet jeans are crumpled on a rock.

It's either a party hat or a ceremonial spear. History hides on the surface of things.

She says, "The Democratic party machine doesn't have as much power as they think in this situation." Above his tie, he nods.

The large white round lights buzz loudly.

The horse bends down and eats the blank grey space above the portrait frame.

In theory, one should own a house in one's political home base.

Cookies and pieces of cake, identified on signs by name and price, sit behind glass in the coffee shop, neither waiting nor not waiting to be eaten.

Choose the profile pic that shows you smiling in a firm-backed posture that isn't common for you.

Story slam.

Outdoors, seen through a glass window, people's actions take on different connotations when accompanied by the soundtrack indoors, so that putting on a bicycle helmet seems like a defiant act of synthesized loneliness.

He says, "You seem a great option in comparison to the other options."

"I like my addiction better than I like you."

The hand reaches across the table and gives the yellow flower to the other hand.

In the mishearing game, the other thinks that what you've said is something much stranger.

What accounts for the way, in one coffee shop, even those who don't know each other seem part of a community, while in another even those sitting together seem alone? Is it only the observer? Yet what if the obvious answer doesn't seem convincing? What if there is some subtlety being communicated in small gestures that the observer can feel and yet not quite notice specifically enough to identify?

Don't worry. Be happy.

He says, "If you give them food and something to do, they don't rebel."

Images of paradise and of hell constitute opposing extremes of the mind filtered through a Christian sensibility that functions as a latent and nearly unrecognized background.

Do I know you?

Finding in a vacant lot the source of the sound: a plastic bag held down by a rock crinkles in the wind.

One can grow tired of hypotheticals.

Construction sites across downtown sit quiet and abandoned on Sundays.

Metal implies motion.

It can appear a relief to recognize that a problem has no solution, but the relief brings new symptoms.

Different kinds of dangers are associated with "out there" and "in here."

Going out to write, he packs his bag with a book, a jacket, a hat, a bottle of water, and forgets only the notebook he has been writing in.

What it's like to vanish: at first the fingers, the hands, the legs, the feet, seem to be moving at a distance, as if all the way across the room. It becomes clear that it was illusion that they were ever attached to some amorphous concept called one's "self," which existed, at best, like a character in a play, constrained by the needs of effective staging. Now the play is over, fading away behind a fog of dry ice. When the fog blows off, the fingers aren't there. The new play begins.

"It's no good to say I can't help it," she says, "because everybody tells me I can."

End Road Work.

One horse stands ready to pull a tourist cart, blinkers over its eyes, leather belt shining with metal studs on its legs, getting petted by a woman in high boots. The other stands at the edge of a fenced field, listening calmly, swishing its tail as two people call it pretty, now and then opening its mouth to nibble at the barbed wire above the fence.

The dead trees, half or more of them blackened, stand above the entangled leafy burgeoning brush.

A written detail is also always a comment on that detail.

Soon enough, the need with which one began seems to fall away, although it can always emerge again.

Bikes with different kinds of engines, some powered by human legs, climb into the mountains and gather again at the barbecue restaurant.

It takes discipline to loiter.

He stands, leaning over a bench, speaking into his empty palm as if there's a phone in it.

The "Service Dog," as the sign on his sweater states, walks past with a proud, erect posture, certain he is going where his people are going.

What is involved in attending to the moment of experience? How does the moment connect to the body and mind experiencing it? Is it a fusion of moment and body? What concept of "moment" is involved? What exists in the time between conceptualization and experience?

Knowing and not knowing.

He pulls the palm hair from the edge of the palm frond and places the frond lightly on the stone wall above the water.

At many moments, the phrases and sentences erase a quickly forgotten thought about sex.

In a gesture against the rhetorical, the rhetorical remains.

Maybe someone should scream.

The aircraft carrier, the flags, the planes on the deck, the sky: the jet roar puts them all back into time.

Two people set out from shore in a rowboat.

Does noticing a place require being partly out of place?

Windows overlook fields, hills, a lake, giving a sense that to be somewhere always feels like it can be repeated when in fact it can't.

The community policed participants aggressively in the name of its own openness.

Beside the bush, the back of a person presses forward against the back of another person.

At the conference, he feels like he'd rather talk to the bus driver.

Eyes inside a car stare as a man walks up into the park along a dirt track coming out of the ravine.

It seems as if someone is raising a hand, asking for help, yet there's no clear reason to interpret the gesture that way.

For those who have never been here before, it's difficult to know how to get to the other side of the road.

The shadow of a tree undulates against the brown slate roof like nothing is the same.

The repeated act of raising the clear glass, which contains a gin and tonic, above the white tablecloth to the sound of ice sloshing.

The power of exhaustion can render meaningless the most tender relationships.

Is the self always shadowed by its own emptiness, always able to feel the ways in which it does not exist?

Leaning on the railing beside tan sand and grayish white boulders, he thinks it is possible to matter.

Shimmering heat cuts into illusions of subjectivity.

"I have always been here before."

Nostalgia seeks the motionless.

Light! An example of phenomena unfolding.

Looking into a building where one almost lived but doesn't, it's possible to imagine what one's life would have been like, living there. Maybe its features wouldn't be much different. Maybe nearly everything that has happened since would have happened differently. How much effect on a pattern does one strand in a pattern have?

Beyond a final row of palm trees, a mountain nearly fades into a blanched sky.

Folded up on its pole, a table umbrella leans against a glass window.

Barefoot in a bikini, she walks up the stairs from the beach, into the road, gets in her car and drives away.

The chain coffee shop has three portraits on the walls, Bob Dylan with a harmonica, Tom Waits with a piano, BB King with a guitar.

"You can take the man out of the Midwest," he says, "but you can't take the Midwest out of the man."

The photo of the wolf pack walking in file through the snow comes with a caption that describes, falsely, the organization of the pack. The caption has been debunked numerous times.

Not looking for the implications of the drama, but for the implications of the non-drama.

A dozen people in their twenties, men and women, circle around a van. One of them, sitting on a bicycle on the edge of the circle, eyes them all skeptically, as if he wishes he was elsewhere.

The heavy gray clouds push in over the palm trees rustling above the farm house.

Beyond the screen, a white pickup with a black gun rack sits beneath a mesquite tree beside a small, yellow adobe house.

The books and bookshelves are not books and bookshelves but a wallpaper design.

The kind of green plastic army men sitting on the shelf in this bar have been owned by boys in the United States for nearly seventy years.

There is a line. Get in it.

Every so often, a restaurant in the neighborhood shuts down before it ever opens.

Notes for a future atmosphere require attention to the present.

Buses bring in groups of schoolchildren to the new open-air plaza in front of the shopping mall.

A helicopter circles the downtown high-rise apartments.

Crane, rooftop, crane, rooftop.

The tree, split in half not far from its base, has two trunks leading in different directions.

A mirror reflection is never the same as the thing it reflects.

The sign above the photo supply store tells people to Do Right, Fear Nothing, Fail Harder, Keep Going.

Five pairs of white socks above five pairs of black sneakers move down the street in a row.

There is no way to stop anything from becoming something else.

They read, off a screen, words of well-known songs they didn't write and sing them as well as they can to the people who crowd the narrow aisles between the tables and the bar.

The wheels of the cars and the legs of the pedestrians and the wind blowing the flags keep the sense of motion constant.

The crossing is over there.

It can be tiring to be one's self all the time.

The longing to be far away is connected to the longing to be closer up.

September 2015 – May 2016

ALSO BY MARK WALLACE

The End of America, Book Three (Glovebox Books, 2018)
Crab (Submodern Books, 2017)
Notes from the Center on Public Policy (Altered Scale Press, 2014)
The End of America, Book One (Dusie Kollectiv, 2012)
The Quarry and The Lot (BlazeVox, 2011)
Felonies of Illusion (Edge Books, 2008)
Walking Dreams: Selected Early Tales (BlazeVox, 2007)
Temporary Worker Rides A Subway (Green Integer, 2004)
Haze: Essays, Poems, Prose (Edge Books, 2004)
Dead Carnival (Avec Books, 2004)
Oh Boy (Slack Buddha Press, 2004)
The Monstrous Failure of Contemplation with *Aquifer* by Kaia Sand (self-publish or perish, 2001)
My Christmas Poem (Poetry New York, 1998)
Nothing Happened and Besides I Wasn't There (Edge Books, 1997)
Sonnets of a Penny-A-Liner (Buck Downs Books, 1996)
In Case of Damage To Life, Limb, or This Elevator (Standing Stones, 1996)
The Haunted Baronet (Primitive Publications, 1996)
The Lawless Man (Upper Limit Music, 1996)
Every Day Is Most Of My Time (Texture Press, 1994)
Complications From Standing In A Circle (Leave Books, 1993)
You Bring Your Whole Life To The Material (Leave Books, 1992)
By These Tokens (Triangle Press, 1990)